MW01088629

READY OR NOT

READY OR NOT

READY OR NOT

PREPARING MEN FOR ALL THAT IS TO COME

CONTENTS

INTRODUCTION

WE PROCLAIM HIM, ADMONISHING EVERY MAN AND
TEACHING EVERY MAN WITH ALL WISDOM, SO THAT
WE MAY PRESENT EVERY MAN COMPLETE IN CHRIST.
COLOSSIANS 1:28

It has been with great joy that I have written this book. I dedicate this book to the churches that I have served and to my precious family. I pray that this will be a devotional resource that the church can use to train disciples so that we may see revival sweep across our nation.

There are many insightful books that you could be reading, but I am honored and excited that you have chosen to read this one. I hope that God will allow you to see into the journey that he has led me on over the last several months. More so than that, I pray that this book would launch you into a journey with God where you begin to see him move in your life and use your life like never before.

I addressed this book to men because I believe that God is shaking the nations and that he is calling men back to biblical truth and action. In my years of ministry, I have been privileged to see men transformed by the gospel. This transformation has had a kingdom impact in their communities, churches, marriages, and in the lives of their children. I have also seen men standing on the edge of transformation. They are unsatisfied with life, they feel useless, and they are longing for more. Some men are convinced that surrendering to Jesus will cost them more than they would gain. Many men are standing on the edge of transformation because they do not have a healthy understanding of the church. They do not see the church as relevant, and that perspective causes them to stand on the sidelines of the church.

Here is the problem: if you don't see the church from the prospective of how God has designed it, then you will miss out on God's mission and calling for your life. Perhaps questions run through your mind like, "Is the church really relevant today? Does God really have a plan for church, and do I really need to be involved?" This book will help clarify God's intent for the church and, ultimately, his intent for your life. The church will ultimately fulfill God's mission.

I have addressed this book to men, but ladies, I do not want you to feel left out. The truths and principles will apply to everyone. I challenge you to dig into the scriptures mentioned in this book. Most of the principles are from Acts 19-20 and the book of Ephesians. I encourage you to read those chapters in Acts and the entire book of Ephesians before you begin this book. There are some Scripture readings and discussion questions at the end of each chapter to help you with individual and group study.

1

READY MEN

PETER SAID TO HIM, "EVEN IF I HAVE TO DIE WITH
YOU, I WILL NOT DENY YOU." ALL THE DISCIPLES SAID
THE SAME THING TOO.

MATTHEW 26:35

The ancient city of Ephesus was a large port city, full of commerce and full of immorality. The Roman city was steeped in Greek mythology and the worship of Roman and Greek gods and goddesses. The town was ruled by not only money and pagan mythology, but by entertainment as well. There was a theater in the center of the city that seated nearly 25,000 people. The theater promoted the city's entertainment industry, which involved athletic events and gladiator games.

This sounds familiar, doesn't it? Our culture centers around money and entertainment. People from all over the known world roamed the streets of Ephesus, which made it a prime place for Paul to start a Christ-centered church. Paul seemed to identify places where people from different walks of life could gather together to worship the one true God. Not only was the city a place where diverse people could gather, but it was also a port city which made it easy to send people to all the known world to share the good news of Jesus. In Acts 18:19, Paul drops off his friends and ministry partners, Aquila and Priscilla, in Ephesus, probably to assess the cultural and spiritual climate. When Paul made his way back to Ephesus, he seemed to be looking for one thing. Where are the God-fearing men?

Isn't that a great question to ask? Where are the God-fearing men in your church or community? Paul began to associate with twelve God-fearing men upon arriving there. These men didn't know all the answers. The beginning of Acts 19 hints that they lacked even knowing Jesus as their master, but these men were ready! They were ready to know Jesus, and they were ready to receive the Holy Spirit and follow Christ wholeheartedly. We come to learn that these were ordinary men, seekers of God, surrendered to Jesus, filled with the Spirit, and committed to discipleship. You most likely think of yourself like these men, just a regular guy trying to seek God. You don't know all the answers, and some of you may not even know Jesus as your master yet. My prayer is that through this book, you will be an ordinary guy who seeks God, who surrenders to Jesus, who is filled with the Spirit, and who is committed to making disciples. Some of you may be thinking, what does all that mean? I plan to unpack all of that along the way.

Paul spent time training these twelve men in the Word of God daily, teaching them about Jesus being the long-awaited Messiah. Like anything in life, you are better equipped for the task if you spend time training. Paul's ministry in Ephesus became the training center for mighty men of faith: future pastors, church planters, people in business, deacons, farmers, trade workers, husbands, and fathers – God-fearing men trained and committed to the cause of Christ.

Is it hard for you to identify God-fearing men in your community or church? Have you ever wondered why these men seem to be so few and far between? I think it is a safe assumption that many communities lack God-fearing men. Consider when Paul arrived in Philippi to establish the church there. Luke records the account in Acts 16:13, "On the Sabbath day they went outside the gate to a riverside, where we were supposing that there would be a place of prayer; and we sat down and began speaking to the women who assembled." Notice that it says the women assembled there. It seems to be that the Philippian community had a lack of God-fearing men, so God established the church in Philippi through a group of God-fearing women. Whether God chooses to use a group of God-fearing men or women, the reality is that people need to be trained in the Word of God so that God's glory can continue to spread to the ends of the earth. This type of training seems very similar to what Jesus did when he called the disciples to follow him.

I find it fascinating that when Jesus called these men, they left everything to follow him; it was as if they had always been anticipating that day. They were *ready* men. He spent years training them, and they were ready to go where Jesus sent them or at least they thought they were ready to follow Jesus anywhere. In Matthew 26:35, Peter declared, "Even if I have to die with you, I will never disown you," and all the disciples said the same. They thought they were ready, but that very night Peter denied even knowing Jesus.

Peter's training wasn't over, and ours isn't either. In our heart of hearts, we may be ready. We may even declare bold things about what we will do for Jesus. However, if we make an honest assessment, our hearts may be ready, but our practice proves otherwise. The disciples longed for the day when their heart's desire and their actions were in one accord.

Isn't this something we all deal with? Take a look at how Paul describes it in Romans 7:15, "For what I am doing, I do not understand; for I am not practicing what I would like to do, but I am doing the very thing I hate." Paul's struggle is the battle that all Christians face. In verse 24, Paul goes on to say, "Wretched man that I am! Who will set me free from the body of this death? Thanks be to God through Jesus Christ our Lord!" Paul knows that this double mindedness is the very thing that Jesus came to work out of us. Peter, the rest of the disciples, and Paul understood this transformation to be a life-long process of preparing, training, and fighting. He knows that victory can only be found in Jesus. Would you say that you are ready to follow Jesus?

STUDY SESSION 1- READY MEN

SCRIPTURE READING – ACTS 19:1-7

1   It happened that while Apollos was at Corinth, Paul passed through the cupper country and came to Ephesus, and found some disciples.

2   He said to them, "Did you receive the Holy Spirit when you believed?" And they said to him, "No, we have not even heard whether there is a Holy Spirit."

3   And he said, "Into what then were you baptized?" And they said, "Into John's baptism."

4   Paul said, "John baptized with the baptism of repentance, telling the people to believe in Him who was coming after him, that is, in Jesus."

5   When they heard this, they were baptized in the name of the Lord Jesus.

6   And when Paul had laid his hands upon them, the Holy Spirit came on them, and they began speaking with tongues and prophesying.

7   There were in all about twelve men.

DISCUSSION QUESTIONS

Do you know any ordinary men, seekers of God, surrendered to Jesus, filled with the Spirit, and committed to discipleship?

Who are they? How has their life impacted others?

The twelve men were committed to being trained in the Word of God for two years. How is this different from how the church is training men today?

What kind of training are you submitting yourself to?

When we consider the life of Peter and the other disciples of Jesus, they were trained by Jesus for three years, but what happened on the night of Jesus' arrest? What does this tell us about training to be a disciple of Jesus?

ADDITIONAL RESOURCES

2

UNTRAINED MEN

NOW AS THEY OBSERVED THE CONFIDENCE OF PETER
AND JOHN AND UNDERSTOOD THAT THEY WERE
UNEDUCATED AND UNTRAINED MEN, THEY WERE
AMAZED, AND BEGAN TO RECOGNIZE THEM AS
HAVING BEEN WITH JESUS.

ACTS 4:13

The twelve men of Ephesus had ready hearts, but
they were not prepared for what was to come. These men
needed to let go of their past and be retrained for what
God had in store. However, that training would not be
without challenges. Paul encountered a group of religious
men in Ephesus who were resistant to the message he was
preaching. On the surface, these men just seemed to be
resisting change, but they were really resisting God. Acts
19:9 says that these men had hardened hearts, were
disobedient, and even spoke evil against Paul and the other
disciples of Jesus. When God-fearing men are trained in the

Scripture and live in obedience to the Word of God, there will be resistance and opposition. Don't let the opposition stop you!

Paul had been training these men in the Jewish synagogue for three months when the resistant men began to speak up. Paul's response to this opposition was to move on. He began meeting with the disciples in a local school. Acts 19:9-10 says that he reasoned daily in the school of Tyrannus for over two years. Neither Paul nor these new disciples were going to let a little resistance slow them down.

Paul understood the importance of moving past resistant men. We should too. It's not that Paul didn't want these men to be believers; he just knew that their hearts were hardened to the message of the gospel. We should continually pray for resistant men. Pray that God would soften their hearts and lead them to repentance. Paul understood that time was of the essence. He was on a mission to train men, and he wasn't going to let any resistance stop him.

When we face opposition, it is easy to feel discouraged. It is no coincidence that Paul later writes a letter to the church in Ephesus, and in the first chapter, he calls the Ephesian believers to remember who they are in Christ. If you ever feel discouraged or defeated, facing resistance in your walk of faith, remember *who* you are and *whose* you are. Let Ephesians 1:3-8 always be a reminder to you:

> "Blessed be the God and Father of our Lord Jesus Christ, who has **blessed us** with every spiritual blessing in the heavenly places in Christ, just as He **chose us** in Him before the foundation of the world, that we would be **holy and blameless** before Him. In love He predestined us to **adoption as sons** through Jesus Christ to Himself, according to the kind intention of His will, to the praise of the glory of His grace, which He freely bestowed on us in the Beloved. In Him **we have redemption** through His blood, the **forgiveness of our trespasses**, according to the riches of His grace

which He lavished on us. In all wisdom and insight."

When we understand who we are, then we are better prepared to live the life that God has called us to live. There is a purpose in everything that God does, and it is important that we figure out our purpose sooner than later. Paul understood that time was of the essence, but he also understood that the time was at hand. If God was going to establish his church in Ephesus, Paul knew that now was the time. In this season of ministry, he had a specific purpose of training men to be leaders of the church.

I believe the time is at hand for God to do a mighty work among men. Have you ever considered what God may have planned for you? Throughout Scripture, we see God speaking to men and women to use them for a particular task.

- We see God calling Abraham to be the father of the nations.

- We see Joseph preserving the life of his Israelite brothers.
- We see Moses being called at the burning bush to set Israel free from slavery.
- We see Esther who was "born for such a time as this" to set Israel free from a death sentence.
- We see Rahab protecting God's people in the face of opposition.
- We see David step in and defeat Goliath and become the king of God's people.

Ultimately, all of these stories in Scripture point us to Jesus, God's only Son. The plan that God has for you will point to Jesus as God's Son as well. I love how the apostle John in his gospel describes Jesus' life culminating in an "hour." The word *hour* is used over 20 times in John's gospel. Take a few moments to read through just a few of these verses from John's gospel.

John 2:4 "And Jesus said to her, "Woman, what does that have to do with us? **My hour has not yet come.**"

John 4:21 "Jesus said to her, "Woman, believe Me, **an hour is coming** when neither in this mountain nor in Jerusalem will you worship the Father."

John 4:23 "**But an hour is coming**, and now is, when the true worshipers will worship the Father in Spirit and truth; for such people the Father seeks to be His worshipers."

John 5:25 "Truly, truly, I say to you, **an hour is coming and now is**, when the dead will hear the voice of the Son of God, and those who hear will live."

John 5:28 "Do not marvel at this; **for an hour is coming**, in which all who are in the tombs will hear His voice."

John 7:30 "So, they were seeking to seize Him; and no man laid his hand on Him, because **His hour had not yet come**."

John 8:20 "These words He spoke in the treasury, as He taught in the temple; and no one seized Him, because **His hour had not yet come**."

John 12:23 "And Jesus answered them, saying, "**The hour has come** for the Son of Man to be glorified."

John 12:27 "Now my soul has become troubled; and what shall I say, 'Father, save Me from this hour? But for this purpose, **I came to this hour**."

John 13:1 "Now before the Feast of the Passover, Jesus knowing that **His hour had come** that He would depart out of this world to the Father, having loved His own who were in the world, He loved them to the end."

John 16:2 "They will make you outcasts from the synagogue, **but an hour is coming** for everyone who kills you to think that he is offering service to God."

John 17:1 "Jesus spoke these things; and lifting up His eyes to heaven, He said, "Father, **the hour has come**; glorify Your Son, that the Son may glorify You."

John 19:14 "Now it was the day of preparation for the Passover; **it was about the sixth hour**. And he said to the Jews, "**Behold, your King!**"

Jesus knew that every hour counted, but he also knew that *the hour* counted. We tend to set aside time for certain things until our calendars are full or overflowing. We make time for godly things such as church attendance, small groups, and daily Bible reading. We set aside a week for the family, youth camp, kid's camp for our children, and summer mission trips. All of these are worthy things, but could there be a better way? Is there a more holistic way to look at our lives and what we do as Christ-followers? With

18

our lives segmented and compartmentalized into semesters and events, weeks and weekends, holidays and vacations, we may tend to focus on what lies ahead instead of *living in the moment*. *Living in the moment* is a whole new mindset for us, and it will take time and effort to break us from our old way of thinking. When we consider training in the Scripture, we must also consider becoming *un*trained in the things that we have become accustomed to doing.

My friend Luke was drafted by the Cubs in the Major League Baseball draft. He is a phenomenal baseball player. In addition to his baseball skills, he is also an avid golfer. If you know anything about a golf swing versus a baseball swing, you know that they are totally different from each other. If you try to play golf with a baseball swing, don't expect to score very well. And if you play baseball with a golf swing, get ready to ride the bench. So, what did my buddy do? Instead of trying to retrain himself to swing a golf club after years of playing baseball, he decided he would just train himself to play golf right-handed so that his left-handed baseball swing would not be at odds with his golf swing. You see, the process of retraining and reforming can be more complicated than building up a whole new foundation. We don't have this luxury in our spiritual journey; we will always be at odds with the old self. This does not mean we should just give up. We might not have the strength, the know-how, or the ability to retrain ourselves. However, God can retrain us. He can renew our minds, and he can give us a new heart; he can make us into a new creation. We must be willing to be untrained, and we must make every effort to give God more than just a moment; we must be intentional about giving God every hour so that he can retrain us.

Minutes make up hours, and seconds make up minutes, but do you know what makes up seconds? Thoughts. God wants to restructure and reform every hour of your day by reshaping your thoughts about every area of life. Ephesians 4:22-23 tells us to lay off the old self and be renewed in the spirit of our mind. If we are going to go through a rigorous training journey, we must lay everything on the table: our time, our talents, our family, our resources, our calling, and our passions. Part of the training process is recognizing that we have had years of ungodly influence, things that have been imposed on us by the culture, things that we have learned from others, and choices that we have made. We must think about how these things affect our everyday lives. Read what God's Word tells us in Jeremiah 1:9-10:

> "Then the LORD stretched out His hand and touched my mouth, and the LORD said to me, "Behold, I have put My words in your mouth. "See, I have appointed you this day over the nations and over the kingdoms, to pluck up and to break down, to destroy and to overthrow, to build and to plant."

The Lord is a builder and a planter, but He isn't interested in building on a faulty foundation or planting in spoiled soil. You cannot retrain yourself. Let God identify, uproot, break down, destroy, and overthrow the evil influences of your past.

Ephesians 5:16 tells us not to walk as unwise men but as wise men making the most of our time because the days are evil. The days may be full of evil, but our hearts, thoughts, actions, and words will not be once they are retrained by God.

In Acts 4:13, it says, "The crowd observed the confidence of Peter and John and understood that they were uneducated and untrained men. They were amazed and began to recognize them as having been with Jesus." You see, the crowd and the culture viewed these men as uneducated and untrained. In reality, these men, and all men today, have been educated and trained. We have all been shaped by our families, friends, careers, choices, and so much more. These men weren't untrained, in fact, they needed to be *untrained* and *retrained* by Jesus.

Can that happen in your life? Sure, it can! Be faithful to live hour by hour following Jesus, and he will transform your life in ways you would never dream. If we are going to be trained by Jesus, the first thing we are going to have to do is stop being resistant! When we give in, fully surrender, and faithfully spend time with Jesus, we will be ready for those big moments when we sense that we were born for such a time as this.

STUDY SESSION 2 – UNTRAINED MEN

SCRIPTURE READING – ACTS 19:8-10

8   And he entered the synagogue and continued speaking out boldly for three months, reasoning and persuading them about the kingdom of God.

9   But when some were becoming hardened and disobedient, speaking evil of the Way before the people, he withdrew from them and took away the disciples, reasoning daily in the school of Tyrannus.

10   This took place for two years, so that all who lived in Asia heard the word of the Lord, both Jews and Greeks.

DISCUSSION QUESTIONS

Have you allowed opposition to stop you from pursuing Jesus? Have you been discouraged by a friend, coworker, family member, or church member?

Is God calling you to step away from a certain person or group of people so that you can pursue him whole heartedly?

What patterns and habits have you established in your life that are going to hinder you from following Jesus?

What does it mean to be *un-trained?* What are some of the areas in your life that need to be *un-trained*?

What was the outcome of their training in verse 10?

How can you use every moment of every day to make much of Jesus?

ADDITIONAL RESOURCES

3

RELIGIOUS MEN

THIS PEOPLE HONORS ME WITH THEIR LIPS,
BUT THEIR HEART IS FAR AWAY FROM ME. BUT IN
VAIN DO THEY WORSHIP ME,
TEACHING AS DOCTRINES THE PRECEPTS OF MEN.
MATTHEW 15:8-9

Training will not be an easy process, and it will
likely look a lot different than the religion you grew up
learning. Christianity, Mormonism, Hinduism, Islam,
Buddhism, Atheism - most likely you have been influenced
by the ideas found in one or more of these religions. Not
only have we been shaped by religion, but the culture
shapes our lives as well. For Paul, it was the Jewish religion
of Judaism. Paul grew up learning the Scripture. He was a
brilliant man who likely had much of the Hebrew Scripture
memorized, but when Paul met Jesus in Acts 9, Paul had to
be retrained in the Scripture. All of his preconceived
notions about the Old Testament had to be done away

with. He would come to understand that the Scripture was not about him trying to achieve righteousness based on merit. Paul's eyes were opened to see that all of the Scripture had been written so that we, as sinful people, could look to Jesus for salvation.

As we journey back to Acts 19, we encounter a bizarre story that should serve as a word of warning for everyone. Acts 19:11 talks about seven religious men who were sons of a Jewish chief priest. In other words, they were steeped in religion. These men noticed that the ministry Paul was doing in the name of Jesus was quite powerful. Paul was becoming a man of influence, and these religious leaders wanted the same status. They decided to try and cast out a demon under the influence of Paul's ministry and in the authority of Jesus. Well, this didn't go so well. "The evil spirit answered and said to them, "I recognize Jesus, and I know about Paul, but who are you? And the man, in whom was the evil spirit, leaped on them and subdued all of them and overpowered them so that they fled out of that house naked and wounded" (Acts 19:15-16).

It is evident that evil is among us; it seems to be a driving force within our culture. Satan, the evil one, lurks in the shadows. His greatest tactics are lies and deception. Paul warns the church about this evil deception. We must heed two warnings from this story. First, do not confuse knowing *about* Jesus with really *knowing* Jesus. These young men in the text were blind because of religion. They had a false sense of security. They thought that because they were Jewish, they would be protected by God. Throughout history, God has provided protection for his people, but that provision only comes through faith in him. Paul was once just like these men, steeped in the Jewish religion, but Jesus brought him out and into the family of God.

In a culture steeped in pagan religion where Roman and Greek gods ruled the day, I find it interesting that Paul points out these seven *Jewish* men. Essentially, these men were professing to worship the same God as

Paul, but their actions proved that they were worshiping themselves.

Perhaps you have been brought up under the banner of Christianity and attend a faithful Bible-believing church, we too need to be warned. The enemy is crafty, and it would be in his best interest to allow you to get close to Jesus and hear about Jesus, being surrounded by followers of Jesus, as long as you never surrender your life to Jesus.

The second warning is do not confuse serving and promoting self with genuine service for Jesus' glory. Just because you are involved in ministry in Jesus' name, it does not mean you are a minister for the glory of Jesus' name. These seven religious men acknowledged Jesus, but they did not serve Jesus. In fact, they call upon Jesus and his disciples to serve them. It's not about what they can do for Jesus; it is about how they could use Jesus to promote themselves. A good word for these men is *counterfeit*. They looked righteous and even had the vocabulary of the righteous. These men tried to fit the gospel into their mold;

what they didn't realize is that Jesus came to break the mold. Jesus cannot be manipulated to fit your agenda. God will expose the counterfeit, and when he does, that which is genuine will come to the forefront.

Jesus confronted this very same mentality with the Pharisees. These men had excellent knowledge of the Word of God, and their intentions were honorable. However, they were blind to how they were supposed to apply the knowledge that they had obtained. Look at what Jesus says about the religious leaders who opposed Him. Matthew 23:1-3 states:

> "Then Jesus spoke to the crowds and to His disciples, saying: "The scribes and the Pharisees have seated themselves in the chair of Moses; therefore all that they tell you, do and observe, but do not do according to their deeds; for they say things and do not do them.""

Jesus knew that religion, even rooted in truth, could mislead people. Do not let religion deceive you; listen to what Jesus says and seek a clear understanding of what

Jesus means for the church to be and do. Bible-believing Christian churches today are not exempt from this. We need to pay careful attention and be on guard about these things. Many people are led through some religious experiences, and they assume that they are in good standing with God. Later in life, many of these same people have a genuine encounter with Jesus that leads to a relationship with God. What do we make of this? Two things are possible. One, their first experience was genuine, and as they matured, they came to a fuller understanding of what took place. Two, Satan convinced them that they were in good standing with God when they were not. This second possibility is startling. There are people who think they are right with God, but they are not. As troubling as this can be, we must remember that God is able to over-rule the deceptive lies of the enemy.

The enemy is at work. He wants to deceive people. He wants us to have a false sense of security in religion, whether it's a false religion or Christianity. If the enemy can make you think you are secure in religion, he will distract

31

you from the actual security that comes only through a relationship with Christ. Men, do not stand on the fringes of religion when God is inviting you into a relationship with him. A relationship with Christ will involve more than just following religious rules. It will involve true repentance that will lead to transformation.

STUDY SESSION 3 – RELIGIOUS MEN

SCRIPTURE READING – ACTS 19:11-17

11   God was performing extraordinary miracles by the hands of Paul,

12   so that handkerchiefs or aprons were even carried from his body to the sick, and the diseases left them and the evil spirits went out.

13   But also some of the Jewish exorcists, who went from place to place, attempted to name over those who had the evil spirits the name of the Lord Jesus, saying, "I adjure you by Jesus whom Paul preaches."

14   Seven sons of one Sceva, a Jewish chief priest, were doing this.

15   And the evil spirit answered and said to them, "I recognize Jesus, and I know about Paul, but who are you?"

16   And the man, in whom was the evil spirit, leaped on them and subdued all of them and overpowered them, so that they fled out of that house naked and wounded.

17   This became known to all, both Jews and Greeks, who lived in Ephesus; and fear fell upon them all and the name of the Lord Jesus was being magnified.

DISCUSSION QUESTIONS

Take a moment to describe your experience with religion.

Have you ever had a religious experience or gone through a religious ritual only to look back on it as meaningless and superficial?

What about the story of the seven Jewish priests stands out to you?

How might people use religion for self-promotion?

What does it look like to do ministry in Jesus' name and for Jesus' fame?

Would you say you have had a religious experience or that you experience Jesus through a growing relationship with him?

ADDITIONAL RESOURCES

4

REPENTANT MEN

THE TIME IS FULFILLED, AND THE KINGDOM
OF GOD IS AT HAND; REPENT AND BELIEVE
IN THE GOSPEL.

MARK 1:15

As Paul was teaching these new disciples in
Ephesus, they went out sharing the gospel in their
community. Something was happening across the city of
Ephesus that can only be explained as the hand of God
upon them. Notice what is repeated in these verses in Acts
19:

> 10 "This took place for two years, so that **all who
> lived in Asia heard the word of the Lord**, both
> Jews, and Greeks."
>
> 17 "**This became known to all, both Jews and
> Greeks**, who lived in Ephesus; and fear fell upon
> them all and the name of the Lord Jesus was being
> magnified."

20 "**So the word of the Lord was growing mightily** and prevailing."

26 "You see and hear that **not only in Ephesus, but in almost all of Asia,** this Paul has persuaded and turned away a considerable number of people."

The message of Jesus was spreading like wildfire in the city and across all of Asia. Notice that this occurs as they face resistance in a culture steeped in pagan worship. So, what? Is this just another news story that spreads across the land like the newest viral video? What's the big deal about the name of Jesus circulating again? Isn't that an old story just getting some news coverage? You see, many people view the message of Jesus as a fad that is here today and gone tomorrow.

In the summer months in south Mississippi, the flies start buzzing around in rural farming areas due to all the cattle. Everyone is always trying the latest trick to keep the flies away. I recently saw that if you put Irish Spring soap out on your deck or in your carport, it would keep the flies away. Maybe this was an ingenious marketing gimmick that Irish Spring circulated on social media — who knows? I did think it was pretty funny when someone posted a picture of a fly sunbathing on a bar of Irish Spring soap. I know it sounds ridiculous but when people are desperate for relief, they will try anything that works.

Here is what everyone wants to know. Does it really work? If it does, where is the evidence? If it's authentic, then the evidence will prove it. I'm not sure if Irish Spring soap keeps flies away, but I am confident that when the message of Jesus spreads, lives will be transformed. Christianity isn't something you can try for a few months. It is the surrender of your entire life. When someone genuinely surrenders to Jesus, there will be evidence in due time. It will be more than a social media fad; it will be a lasting transformation. You can see the evidence of lives being changed in Acts 19:18-20:

> "Many also of those who had believed kept
> coming, confessing and disclosing their practices.
> And many of those who practiced magic brought

their books together and began burning them in
the sight of everyone; they counted up the price
of them and found it fifty thousand pieces of
silver. So the word of the Lord was growing
mightily and prevailing."

Don't overlook what took place here. They *listened* to the
gospel of salvation and *believed* it, and they were *sealed*
with the Holy Spirit of promise (Ephesians 1:13). The result
was a total confession and abandonment of sinful living.
These people were making their living through mystic
religion that involved all sorts of magic and the following of
religious rule books. Take note that these people brought
their books of magic which would have been worth a small
fortune, and they burned them! These new Christians were
willing to burn their old way of life in order to live fully in
their newfound relationship with Jesus.

There are so many professing Christians still
holding on to areas of sin in their life that they need to let
die – habits, addictions, relationships, jobs, and hobbies.

True repentance involves not just acknowledging sin but also confessing sin and disclosing sin.

Often when we look at the Scripture, we try to discern if the passage is *describing* what took place or if it is *prescribing* a specific pattern by which we should live. I encourage you to let the passage above be a prescription that you implement into your life. There is great freedom for Christ-followers when they fully confess their sin and disclose their practices in front of other Christians.

We have become so embarrassed and private with our sin that we are not experiencing freedom from it. Notice that it says they burned their books "in the sight of everyone." Even before Jesus began his ministry, the people were led to confess their sins. I believe that is one reason his ministry spread so rapidly. The calling of John the Baptist was to prepare the way for Jesus, and he did it by calling people to confess their sins. Matthew 3:5-6 states:

> "Then Jerusalem was going out to him, and all Judea and all the district around the Jordan; and

> they were being baptized by him in the Jordan
> River, as they confessed their sins."

In your Christian journey, find a group of men or form a group where people can be open about their sin. Christians are people of light and truth. Sin hides in the shadows; however, sin loses its power when it is brought into the light. James 5:16 states:

> "Therefore, confess your sins to one another and
> pray for one another so that you may be healed.
> The effective prayer of a righteous man can
> accomplish much."

Confessing sin one to another seemed to be the practice for Christians in the early church. For some reason, open confession seems to be the fad that sadly faded out. Perhaps this lack of confession is another area where the enemy is trying to cripple God's people and stifle the growth of the church. Consistent confession of sins to one another opens the door for accountable living. When Christians acknowledge their sin in front of others, it paves the way for helping others see their sin.

Christians usually have no problem identifying sin in others, but approaching people about their sin can be difficult. Still, pointing out sin is the most loving thing we can do when we do it with the right motive and from a heart of genuine love. It has been said that we should tend the weeds in our own garden, meaning that we should pay attention to our own sin. Yet sometimes we cannot tell the difference between fruit-bearing plants and weeds, so we need to get an outside opinion.

King David found himself entangled in sin when he took Uriah's wife to be his own. He covered up and rationalized his sin to the point that he hid it from others and himself. He suppressed the truth and did not deal with his sin. However, God stepped in and sent a man named Nathan to help David see his sin. David was being led to repentance. The Bible teaches us that the kindness of the Lord brings us to repentance. Nathan stepping into David's life was an act of God's kindness! You need kind people in your life, and you need to be a friend that shares God's kindness to those you love.

When Jesus raised Lazarus from the dead, he called his name, and Lazarus came forth from among the tomb still wrapped in his grave clothes from head to toe. The passage in John 11:42 tells us that even his face was covered. Spiritually speaking, Lazarus was alive, but he was still covered in his grave clothes. Many Christians live their lives this way. They have heard Jesus call their name, and they are alive, but they appear to be dead. I love what Jesus says to the crowd around Lazarus. In John 11:44, he tells them, "You unbind him, and let him go." *They* unwrapped the garments. *The people* around Lazarus participated in his freedom.

You and I need people around us to step into our lives to help us see our sin and unbind our grave clothes. Paul says it well in Ephesians 4:25-32. Before you can put on the garments of righteousness, you have to take off some garments of immorality. Praise be to God for his Son who has called us out of the tomb and brought us from death to life!

We must see that God has a process for removing the grave clothes, and it involves his Word, his Spirit, and his people. When you are concerned about a fellow Christian's sinful actions, before you call them out in their sin, try to approach them with confession of your own sin. What happens when God's people confess sin to one another and call each other out of sin? They live lives of true repentance, and the Word of the Lord grows mightily and prevails across the land.

STUDY SESSION 4 – REPENTANT MEN

SCRIPTURE READING – ACTS 19:18-20

18   Many also of those who had believed kept coming, confessing and disclosing their practices.

19   And many of those who practiced magic brought their books together and began burning them in the sight of everyone; and they counted up the price of them and found it fifty thousand pieces of silver.

20   So the word of the Lord was growing mightily and prevailing.

DISCUSSION QUESTIONS

How did the people respond to the message of Paul in verse 18?

What does it mean to confess and disclose one's practices to another?

How do you feel about publicly confessing your sin with others who are willing to do the same?

What happened as a result of their confession? Do you think we would see the same result today?

Do you think these verses should serve as a pattern for Christians to live by?

ADDITIONAL RESOURCES

5

DISTURBED MEN

FOR THE WORD OF THE CROSS IS FOOLISHNESS
TO THOSE WHO ARE PERISHING,
BUT TO US WHO ARE BEING SAVED
IT IS THE POWER OF GOD.

1 CORINTHAINS 1:18

When the Word of God begins to permeate the culture, it will be followed by a holy disturbance. What is a holy disturbance? When God's Word goes forth, it goes forth as a beacon of truth that shines a light on the sin and evil within the culture. This means that it shines a light to expose people's sin. This type of disturbance has two primary responses. The first is that people repent of their sin. The second is that people are disturbed by the Word of God, and they try to cause a bigger disturbance to shut down the progress of the gospel. Paul understood this well, because he could recall a time in his own life where he tried to cause a disturbance to shut-down the gospel.

Acts 19:23-41 introduces us to a silversmith named Demetrius. He made his living forming idols of the goddess Artemis and selling them to the people of Ephesus so they could worship her. The expansion of Christianity threatened Demetrius' prosperity. If people turned to worship Jesus, they would in turn abandon their worship of Artemis, which meant that they would have no need for Demetrius' silver idols.

The gospel will disturb people, and we need to understand that disturbed people cause disturbances. Although what was happening in Ephesus seemed like a disturbance to many people, the Christians knew genuine revival was sweeping across the land. Demetrius was trying to extinguish the fires of revival, but he was really fanning the flame. Christians need to know that disturbances are going to come because many people feel threatened by the gospel. The gospel exposes sin and sinful living, and not everyone is ready to deal with sin.

Mike is a faithful deacon in our church who is involved in several ministry areas. He has spent a good bit of time sharing the gospel in the local jail. One day when he entered the jail to share the gospel, he said that one of the inmates would immediately go to the bathroom and start flushing the toilet over and over so that he and the other inmates could not hear the Word of God. Mike said he just preached louder so that the others could listen to the message.

Mike mentioned another instance where he entered the jail to see an intimidating man he had never seen before sitting and waiting for him to arrive. A massive scar across his face and neck made Mike a bit uneasy. At the end of the gospel presentation, the man said he wanted to be saved, so Mike led him to the Lord.

When Mike was walking out, the man hollered at him across the room and said, "I am sorry!" Mike turned and looked at him and said, "You just made things right with the Lord; you do not owe me an apology." He said, "Sir, yes I do! For the last several weeks, you have been coming in here, and I have hated your guts." Mike replied, "You have been here for weeks?" He was confused because this was the first time they had met. He said, "Yes sir, every week when I'd see you coming, I'd go to my bunk, and I'd put my blanket over my head so I wouldn't have to listen to you. You just kept coming week after week. I'm getting ready to go to Parchman Prison, and something just made me get up and come and listen to you. I am sorry that I hated you."

The Word of God is foolishness to those that are perishing. If you spend a moment comparing Demetrius, the toilet flusher, the scar-faced inmate, and the apostle Paul, you will see that they all have pretty similar stories. They all were disturbed by the Word of God. The only difference is that the latter two were captured by God's grace and surrendered to Christ by faith.

Christians tend to separate themselves from the world by forgetting that they were once entrenched in the world. If you are a Christian, you should never lose sight that you were once dead in your trespasses and sins, walking according to the course of this world. We must remember that *God* has made us alive *in Christ* and saved us by *his* grace (Ephesians 2:8).

Does that sound familiar? It's no coincidence that Paul wrote that in his letter to the church in Ephesus. Jesus died and gave his life for disturbed men, so let us pray fervently for them. Better yet, Jesus doesn't want us to have an "us versus them" mentality. Jesus died for all! Period! End of the story! May we rejoice with those who have come to understand God's gift of salvation. May we be prayerfully patient with those who are disturbed by the gospel.

After the disturbance in Ephesus ended, Paul gathered the disciples and encouraged them to continue the ministry work, and he moved on to another region to continue ministry. In a first glance reading of the text, it may seem that Paul abandoned the Ephesian church when things got difficult. If you read more about Paul's story, you will find out that he was always willing to face adversity head-on. Paul set out to encourage the believers in

Macedonia. However, he did not leave the Ephesian church orphaned or without a leader.

STUDY SESSION 5 – DISTURBED MEN

SCRIPTURE READING – ACTS 19:23-27

23 About that time there occurred no small disturbance concerning the Way.

24 For a man named Demetrius, a silversmith, who made silver shrines of Artemis, was bringing no little business to the craftsmen;

25 these he gathered together with the workmen of similar trades, and said, "Men, you know that our prosperity depends upon this business.

26 "You see and hear that not only in Ephesus, but in almost all of Asia, this Paul has persuaded and turned away a considerable number of people, saying that gods made with hands are no gods at all.

27 "Not only is there danger that this trade of ours fall into disrepute, but also that the temple of the great goddess Artemis be regarded as worthless and that she whom all of Asia and the world worship will even be dethroned from her magnificence."

DISCUSSION QUESTIONS

How does the gospel threaten people's way of life?

Why was Demetrius so disturbed by the gospel that Paul was preaching?

What do people do who are disturbed by the gospel?

What part of your life is being threatened by the gospel? What will your response be?

Does your life reflect the gospel in such a way that people seemed disturbed by your faith?

Additional Resources

6

SPIRIT-FILLED MEN

YOU WILL RECEIVE POWER WHEN THE HOLY SPIRIT COMES UPON YOU AND YOU WILL BE MY WITNESSES...

ACTS 1:8

When Paul first arrived at Ephesus, he gathered twelve God-fearing men who were followers of John the Baptist. This meant that they were baptized in a baptism of repentance, but they had not heard the full story about Jesus dying to save people from their sins. As Paul taught them, they became followers of Jesus filled with the Holy Spirit. During the two years Paul spent training these men, he wasn't just giving these men information. He was teaching them how to listen to the Spirit of God and how to walk by the Spirit of God. He taught them to allow the Spirit to teach them the Scripture and reveal the truth to them. He taught them how the Holy Spirit would convict them of sin and lead them into holy living. He taught them about the Holy Spirit empowering them to be a witness. He was helping them understand their spiritual gifts so that they could put their gifts into action.

Paul was very familiar with living a life transformed and led by the Spirit. Paul knew that the church needed to understand the role of the Holy Spirit in their lives! Notice what he prays for in Ephesians 3:14-19:

> "For this reason I bow my knees before the Father, from whom every family in heaven and on earth derives its name, that He would grant you, according to the riches of His glory, to be strengthened with power through His Spirit in the inner man, so that Christ may dwell in your hearts through faith; and that you, being rooted and grounded in love, may be able to comprehend with all the saints what is the breadth and length and height and depth, and to know the love of Christ which surpasses knowledge, that you may be filled up to all the fullness of God."

Paul knew that the Holy Spirit would continue to lead the church. He knew that God had equipped the believers with spiritual gifts, and if those gifts were used, God would continue to do his work in Ephesus and the surrounding area.

Paul later wrote to the church, reminding them about spiritual gifts in Ephesians 4:11-13:

> "And He gave some as apostles, and some as prophets, and some as evangelists, and some as pastors and teachers for the equipping of the saints for the work of service, to the building up of the body of Christ; until we all attain to the unity of the faith, and of the knowledge of the Son of God, to a mature man, to the measure of the stature which belongs to the fullness of Christ."

It is vitally important for the church to be aware of spiritual gifts and to use those gifts to build up the body of Christ. Paul lays out leadership gifts within the church in this text, but he also gives the purpose for those gifts. Notice that the leadership gifts in the church should result in the saints being equipped for service. Paul is very strategic in talking about the leadership gifts. He knows that the church will not effectively accomplish its mission if the leadership loses its focus.

Churches often fall into a trap where they create a ministry structure that can only reach a certain capacity. It has no room for growth. Church leaders fall into the trap of only serving people and never equipping people to serve. It doesn't take very long for the *always serving* and *never equipping* mindset to create an unhealthy culture within a church. When pastors and teachers spend all of their time serving the people, you can liken it to a parent who always picks up after a child. As the child grows, he or she will have a sense of entitlement, a lack of responsibility, a lack of self-worth and value, and a lack of ownership and work ethic.

Many churches are functioning this way, and the church's leadership may be enabling this type of mindset within the congregation. For many churches, there has to be a paradigm shift. Church leaders must learn to equip people instead of only serving people. Pastors and teachers must understand that their greatest act of service to the church is to equip the believers for service. It won't be easy for a congregation, but this shift in mindset must take place for the church to be healthy. This shift in mindset may mean that certain ministries have to stop until people can lead and train to serve. The church will have to abandon the mindset that says, "We have always done it that way, or that's why we pay the pastor." Pastors must help people see their spiritual gifts and call them to serve using those gifts.

If your church's ministries are started and held together by your pastor's leadership, don't be surprised when your pastor is called somewhere else or called to his heavenly home that the ministries of your church leave with him. Paul had worked tirelessly to spread the gospel and equip believers for service. He was a drifter, but he kept in close touch with believers across the many places where he stopped on his missionary journeys. I love what he says to Barnabas in Acts 15:36:

"After some days, Paul said to Barnabas, "Let us return and visit the brethren in every city in which we proclaimed the word of the Lord, and see how they are."

Paul had a care and concern for all the people that he served and trained in ministry. His love was authentic. He always desired to be with them and to encourage them. The Holy Spirit was leading Paul to leave Ephesus to oversee another area of ministry. Paul knew that he was leaving them in the hands of the greatest leader of all – the Holy Spirit within them. Men and women of faith in Ephesus not only had the Holy Spirit to guide them, but they also had their newfound faith family to lean on. This faith family was a community like they had never experienced before. Paul encouraged the church in Ephesians 5 to be filled with the Holy Spirit. He also gave some results of being Spirit-filled.

Pastors and teachers who equip their people for serving in the kingdom will find great delight in watching God work through the people he has called them to shepherd. Paul called the church that he helped start in Philippi his joy and his crown! In Galatians 6:6, Paul calls the church to share all good things with the one who teaches him. Pastors, equip your people and enjoy watching them use their gifts! Church members, encourage your pastors with what God is doing in and through your lives as you live led by the Holy Spirit. Many church members view their church as being unhealthy, but very few members of churches are digging in to address the issues. Some churches have open wounds that stem from years of neglect. The church isn't a business that needs a good CEO. It is a body that needs constant care and attention to be healthy.

Health is hard to get back once you lose it, but it is also hard to maintain once you have it. To live healthy lives, we have to set aside things that *we want to do* for something that *we must do*. The body of Christ must do the same. If we are going to have Spirit-led churches, we must be Spirit-filled men.

Spirit-filled men must understand that the Holy Spirit is the person of God indwelling within them and speaking to them. Many people view the Holy Spirit as a force or an influence that gives them a nudge or a prompt. However, we must seek to understand the leadership of the Holy Spirit in our life as the very person of God speaking to us. When we limit our view of the Holy Spirit as a force or influence, then we likely treat his leadership like a suggestion to live by rather than a command to obey. The Holy Spirit becomes the master of Spirit-filled men and Spirit-filled churches. Will you set aside your preferences and surrender to the Holy Spirit's leadership? Will you choose to be a church member who shares the load? Be trained in the Word, be constant in prayer, serve in your gifts, evangelize the lost, and worship God wholeheartedly.

STUDY SESSION 6 – SPIRIT FILLED MEN

SCRIPTURE READING – EPHESIANS 3:14-19

14   For this reason I bow my knees before the Father,

15   from whom every family in heaven and on earth derives its name,

16   that He would grant you, according to the riches of His glory, to be strengthened with power through His Spirit in the inner man,

17   so that Christ may dwell in your hearts through faith; and that you, being rooted and grounded in love,

18   may be able to comprehend with all the saints what is the breadth and length and height and depth,

19   and to know the love of Christ which surpasses knowledge, that you may be filled up to all the fullness of God.

20   Now to Him who is able to do far more abundantly beyond all that we ask or think, according to the power that works within us,

21   to Him be the glory in the church and in Christ Jesus to all generations forever and ever. Amen.

DISCUSSION QUESTIONS

What does Paul pray for in his letter to the church in Ephesus?

Have you tried to conquer sin by your own strength and power? What was the result?

Can you see the evidence of the Holy Spirit in your life? Can others see the evidence?

Do you view the Holy Spirit as a person or as a force?

Are you aware of your Spiritual-giftedness?

Additional Resources

7

ADOPTED MEN

BECAUSE YOU ARE SONS, GOD HAS SENT FORTH THE
SPIRIT OF HIS SON INTO OUR HEARTS,
CRYING, "ABBA! FATHER!"

GALATIANS 4:6

Because the culture does not look to God's Word to define the church, the church has become under-valued and misunderstood. However, this misunderstanding does not just exist within the culture, but it has trickled its way into the church itself. Now is the time for believers to truly understand God's design and intent for the church. Back in chapter two, I reminded you about a Christian's identity in Christ. Those reminders were things like you are called, you are redeemed, and you are chosen. I want to expound on one of those privileges that is often overlooked. In Ephesians 1:5, Paul says that believers are predestined to adoption as sons through Jesus Christ to himself.

Adoption is beautiful. It is when someone who was cast out and abandoned gets welcomed into the family; they once had no inheritance, but now they share in an inheritance. I was sitting with an elderly lady recently when the conversation about adoption came up. She said she could remember her grandmother saying, "For someone to adopt was the most Christian thing that someone could do." I think she understood something that few people understand about adoption. Theologian J.I. Packer said it well when he said, "The entire Christian life has to be understood in terms of adoption." I went on to tell the older lady the following story about adoption.

Laurie is a faithful Christian lady who began praying for a young couple who didn't have any children, and they were considering adoption. Laurie was scheduled to have lunch with her old college roommate, Dinah. They had not seen each other in several years. Little did she know that God was about to reveal the answer to her prayers. Over lunch, Laurie and Dinah were catching up on life when Dinah mentioned to Laurie that there was a little nine-month-old girl in her community being put up for adoption. The little girl had been in a bad situation where the mother and father were no longer in the picture. There were several families from the community interested in adopting the little girl. Laurie spoke up and gave Dinah the name of the young couple who she had been praying for, and she didn't think much else about it. Several weeks went by, and on a Sunday afternoon after church, Laurie received a phone call that shocked her. Dinah had taken the name of the couple to the little girl's guardian, and she called and wanted to know if the couple was still interested in adoption. Laurie was overwhelmed because she had not even told the couple about giving out their names. She told Dinah that she would call the couple and get back to her.

You see, this is not just some adoption story. This is the story about how God added to my family. It was Laurie, the sweet faithful prayer warrior from my church, calling my phone. She left me a voicemail that said she had urgent news, but good news, and to call her back as soon as possible. My wife and I anxiously made our way to

Laurie's home, because she wanted to tell us the news in person. We were speechless when Laurie told us about the phone call that she had received earlier that afternoon.

We didn't sleep a wink that night! My wife and I met baby Gracie two weeks later. Shortly after, we received temporary custody until we completed the adoption process about a year later. Our little Gracie was a gift that we didn't deserve or earn, and that is what God's grace is to us – an undeserved gift.

I share this story of God's amazing grace for two reasons. First, I want you to see that God cares about the details of your life and the desires of your heart. Secondly, I want you to see how God used his people to accomplish his will. I remember a specific time where I shared with Laurie and other church members that we wanted them to pray about our family. My wife and I longed to have children, but we had not been able to conceive. I also remember standing in my living room as my wife was looking up adoption agencies. I said a passing prayer, "God, you don't have to use an adoption agency if you don't want to." God answered my prayer using his faithful praying people. As we walked through the adoption process, God let us experience first-hand what it means for us to be adopted into his family. God is adopting people into his family every day through faith in his one and only Son. There is no greater gift of grace than God giving his Son, Jesus! John 1:12 tells us, "But as many as received Him, to them He gave the right to become children of God, even to those who believe in His name."

My wife and I were running an after-school program in our community when Gracie moved into our home. Many of the children that we worked with had questions about why we were taking care of Gracie. My wife shared with one of the boys about adoption, and he looked up and asked her, "Is that the Christian thing to do?" We thought that it was a fascinating question. For some people, yes, it is absolutely the most Christian thing to do. Men, we must always remember God adopting us into his family is our highest honor and greatest privilege. J.I. Packer also said this about adoption, "It is the highest privilege that the gospel offers." I hope you can see that adoption is very dear to God's heart.

Through adoption, you have a new father, God. You have a new family, the church. I can tell you through first-hand experience that God is working miracles in and through his church! I believe God put our adoption story in motion long ago, but I think it was made a reality the day I opened up to our church family and asked them to begin praying. In Ephesians 3, Paul reminds us that his *manifold* wisdom would be made known through the church. God plans to reveal himself through the church. If you want to see God move and experience God-sized things, you need to connect to a local Bible-believing church.

The word *manifold* mentioned in the above verse means multicolored. In other words, God has so much that he wants to reveal to us about his character and goodness, but we fail to see it because we don't have a healthy view of the church. Most men are not fully committing to the church! Don't spend your life on the fringes of the church. Many people have a very limited view of God and what he is doing in the world. When we fail to see the church like God intends, we are choosing to be spiritually color blind when God wants us to see him in full color. God is not only accomplishing something in this world through his church, but he is also proving his grandness to the rulers and authorities in the heavenly places through his church (Ephesians 3:10).

If you are a Christian, God's desire to use you in his family mission should light a fire in you! You mean to tell me that God wants to use *us* to manifest *his* glory in the heavenly places! Yes, that is what his Word is telling us. Paul closes his prayer in Ephesians 3 with these words: "Now to him who is able to do far more abundantly beyond all that we ask or think, according to the power that works within us, to Him be glory in the *church* and in *Christ Jesus* to all generations forever and ever. Amen!"

Men, if your purpose in life is to give God glory, you need to be connected and involved in the local church. Don't have this mentality that says, "I love Jesus, but I don't love the church." Jesus died for the church; the church is his bride. If you love Jesus then you learn to love and be a contributing member of a local church. Why? Because God is glorified in his church and in his Son.

STUDY SESSION 7 – ADOPTED MEN

SCRIPTURE READING – EPHESIANS 1:1-6

1   Paul, an apostle of Christ Jesus by the will of God, To the saints who are at Ephesus and who are faithful in Christ Jesus:

2   Grace to you and peace from God our Father and the Lord Jesus Christ.

3   Blessed be the God and Father of our Lord Jesus Christ, who has blessed us with every spiritual blessing in the heavenly places in Christ,

4   just as He chose us in Him before the foundation of the world, that we would be holy and blameless before Him. In love

5   He predestined us to adoption as sons through Jesus Christ to Himself, according to the kind intention of His will.

6   to the praise of the glory of His grace, which He freely bestowed on us in the Beloved.

DISCUSSION QUESTIONS

How would you describe the family you grew up in? How were you influenced in both positive and negative ways?

Take a moment to think about the life of an orphan. What do they long for? Have you ever longed for these things?

What does it mean to be adopted by God, and how should that impact our lives?

As children of God, we are his representatives. What kind of weight should this truth carry in our lives?

What does adoption teach us about how God views the church? How should this impact our view of the church?

ADDITIONAL RESOURCES

8

CALLED MEN

THEREFORE I, THE PRISONER OF THE LORD,
URGE YOU TO WALK IN A MANNER
WORTHY OF THE CALLING WITH WHICH YOU
HAVE BEEN CALLED

EPHESIANS 4:1

The moment when our ambition and actions align with God's desires is the moment we begin to live. At the heart of Paul's letter to the church in Ephesus, Paul expresses his desire for them to live according to their calling. One of the significant thematic words that appears throughout the letter is the word *walk*. Paul used this word thirty times in his writings and eight times in seven verses within the book of Ephesians.

Eph 2:2 "...in which **you formerly walked** according to the course of this world, according to the prince of the power of the air, of the Spirit that is now working in the sons of disobedience."

Eph 2:10 "For we are His workmanship, created in Christ Jesus for good works, which God prepared beforehand so that we would **walk in them**."

Eph 4:1 "Therefore I, the prisoner of the Lord, implore you to **walk in a manner worthy** of the calling with which you have been called,"

Eph 4:17 "So, this I say, and affirm together with the Lord, that you **walk no longer just as the Gentiles** also walk, in the futility of their mind,"

Eph 5:2 "...and **walk in love**, just as Christ also loved you and gave Himself up for us, an offering and a sacrifice to God as a fragrant aroma."

Eph 5:8 "...or you were formerly darkness, but now you are Light in the Lord; **walk as children of Light**."

Eph 5:15-16 "Therefore, **be careful how you walk**, not as unwise men but as wise, making the most of your time because the days are evil."

God wants you to use your spiritual gifts to fulfill your spiritual calling. Many people are aware that God has a calling, but they are not sure what that calling means for their life. For some reason, people continue to live day after day, year after year, just hoping that they are fulfilling their calling. All the while, they live with a strong sense of discontent. They are not fulfilled or satisfied. God is not just in the business of pulling the sin out of you. He wants to put something *within* you so that his power can flow from you.

While some people are entirely unaware of their calling, others are simply distracted in their calling. Here are some absolutes when it comes to everyone's God-ordained calling.

God's calling for you...

- Will be centered around faith in Jesus
- Will express your Spiritual giftedness
- Will mature you in Christ-likeness
- Will be rooted in the truth of Scripture
- Will build the church through unity
- Will expand the kingdom of God in the world

Pastor Tony Evans defines God's calling for each person's life in this way: "The customized life purpose that God has ordained for you to accomplish in order to bring him the greatest glory and the maximum expansion of his kingdom." When Jesus called the disciples, he called them out of a particular lifestyle into a new one. He called Peter, James, John, and Andrew out of fishing to become fishers of men. Levi and Zacchaeus were called from being greedy tax collectors to being generous givers. He called Paul from preserving the Jewish religion and heritage to promoting Christianity to the Gentiles. Just as Jesus called these men, there is a call on your life too. The purpose of everyone's calling will be the same, to make much of Jesus in the world. How he wants you to do that will be up to him and how you respond to him.

When you follow Jesus, everything is on the table for him to take over and take the lead. He may call you to simply reorient your life to have a change in perspective. He may lead you to abandon some of the things in your life: relationships, career, hobbies, or possibly even where you live.

Paul tells the church in Ephesus to remember that they were once dead in their trespasses and sins. Paul knew what that meant. Paul had some pretty grievous sin in his life. He desired to have Christians arrested and had Christians killed at one point. When you pull back the layers of Paul's sinfulness, you can see that Paul had a murderous spirit because he had an idol that he worshiped. Paul's skewed understanding of Scripture was that he was required to preserve the Jewish people and their religion at all costs. He thought he was serving God when he was actually serving an idol. Upon meeting Jesus, Paul's perspective on Scripture changed because the object of his worship changed. Paul had all the same knowledge, but he gained the wisdom to accompany his knowledge through obedience to Jesus. Likewise, Peter was a fisherman by trade, but upon meeting Jesus, his skills, work ethic, and ability shifted toward winning souls for Jesus.

The aim of our calling is the same, but the practice will be different for each of us. You will have to determine if God wants you to abandon things or to use those very things for his glory. God's calling on my life is to teach the Word of God and to equip the local church for ministry. I am also an avid outdoorsman. I enjoy hunting, fishing, and playing golf. Over the years, and still, to this day, my passion for the outdoors can distract me from my calling. I now realize that God can use my passion for the outdoors if I am willing to have the proper perspective.

Over the years, I have attempted to leverage my passions for kingdom purposes. I have organized golf tournaments to raise money for missions. I have done fishing events for children, youth, and men with the intent of sharing Jesus with them. I have turned my passion for archery hunting into a men's small group that encourages men to be the husbands and fathers that God has called them to be. I enjoy doing all of these things with the new aim of making Jesus known. I still have times in my life where those passions and hobbies become idols. I have to constantly remind myself of Ephesians 5:15-16, that I am to no longer walk in the futility of my mind, but I am to walk like a wise man making the most of my time because the days are evil.

You have to figure out God's calling for you, and you have to walk in that calling if you are going to be fulfilled in this life. I love the story in Mark 5:1-20. Jesus has made his way to the country of the Gerasenes, where he finds a man possessed by demons living among the tombs. Jesus cast out the demons and healed the man. After Jesus healed the man, all the people of the country of the Gerasenes and the surrounding district asked Jesus to leave them. The demon-possessed man begged Jesus to let him follow him. This man wanted to follow Jesus to other places to go and share his story with the rest of the world. Yet, Jesus told him, "Return to your house and describe what great things God has done for you, and how he had mercy on you. And he went away and began to proclaim in Decapolis what great things Jesus had done for him; and everyone was amazed."

Essentially, Jesus told the man that his calling was to be faithful in his local city. I have called you from among the tombs to go into the city's streets. The man didn't walk away sad because he couldn't go with Jesus. He walked away being obedient to his God-given calling. Be all in where Jesus has you. If you're not sure about your calling, stay faithful in serving Jesus where you are until he reveals more to you about your calling.

The word Decapolis is a term that represents ten Gentile cities. It is very likely that this man went to those cities telling everyone about what Jesus had done for him. Notice their response: "Everyone was amazed." The very people who rejected Jesus while he was in that city were now amazed at what Jesus had done for this man. In Mark 7:31-35, Jesus returns to the Decapolis. This time, the people did not ask Jesus to leave; they asked him to heal their sick. Could it be possible that the demonic man's testimony prepared the people's hearts to receive Jesus? What if the man insisted on traveling with Jesus instead of being obedient to Jesus' command to stay home and be a witness? You see, every one of Jesus' followers has a calling, and each calling is different. We need to know that people may not be willing to receive Jesus if we do not fulfill our calling.

If I had to write the Christian calling down in one simple statement, it would be what Jesus told the man in Mark 5:19: "Go, report to them what great things the Lord has done for you, how he had mercy on you." I don't know what God's calling is on your life. Whether that is to be like Simon Peter, dropping his nets to go anywhere that Jesus called him, to be like Paul, providing the gospel to the Gentile people, or to be like this man who was called to stay home and be a witness in his community. God desires for you to live in your calling. He isn't hiding your calling from you, so quit hiding from your calling.

STUDY SESSION 8 – CALLED MEN

SCRIPTURE READING – EPHESIANS 4:1-8

1   Therefore I, the prisoner of the Lord, implore you to walk in a manner worthy of the calling with which you have been called,

2   with all humility and gentleness, with patience, showing tolerance for one another in love,

3   being diligent to preserve the unity of the Spirit in the bond of peace.

4   There is one body and one Spirit, just as also you were called in one hope of your calling;

5   one Lord, one faith, one baptism,

6   one God and Father of all who is over all and through all and in all.

7   But to each one of us grace was given according to the measure of Christ's gift.

8   Therefore it says "WHEN HE ASCENDED ON HIGH, HE LED CAPTIVE A HOST OF CAPTIVES, AND HE GAVE GIFTS TO MEN."

DISCUSSION QUESTIONS

According to Paul, what will your calling entail?

Of the things listed, which ones are the most difficult for you to practice?

Who do you know that has pursued God's call on their life?

Do you have a holy ambition, a sense of calling or obligation that God has put on your heart?

Are you sure of your spiritual gift? Are you using it in ministry?

Have you been hiding from your calling?

ADDITIONAL RESOURCES

9

MATURE MEN

FINALLY THEN, BRETHREN, WE REQUEST AND
EXHORT YOU IN THE LORD JESUS, THAT AS YOU
RECEIVED FROM US INSTRUCTION AS TO HOW YOU
OUGHT TO WALK AND PLEASE GOD (JUST AS YOU
ACTUALLY DO WALK), THAT YOU EXCELL STILL MORE

1 THESSALONIANS 4:1

Ephesians 4:15 mentions that believers in Christ
are to grow and mature. Paul uses the phrase "to grow up
in all aspects into Christ." What does it mean to grow up
into all aspects? It means that you choose to walk in your
calling, constantly learning and doing what is pleasing to
the Lord. Paul describes this type of living in Ephesians
4:17-5:21. Maturing as a believer means that you not only
know what God has called you *from*, but you also know
what God has called you *to*.

Paul reminds the church in Ephesus of who they
were before knowing Christ. In Ephesians 4:18, Paul tells

them that they were excluded from the life of God because of the ignorance that was in them, because of the hardness of their hearts. For people to live their lives excluded from the life of God – what a tragedy that would be! Many people are living their lives that way. Have you been living the life that God intends for you to live? The good news is that you don't have to live your life without Christ and his purpose. You can trust and grow in Christ so that you can live the life God intended for you to live. A mature man abandons his old life to live the life God intended for him to live.

Mature men are not men who have their whole life in order. Mature men are men who choose to take the next right step. According to Ephesians 5:1, mature men strive to imitate God, which means that they strive to be so closely connected to Jesus that the attributes and character of Jesus begin to fill their minds and be shown through their actions. Mature men know that every area of their lives will be shaped and formed by Jesus, and they welcome that. As you mature in Christ, your thoughts, attitude, speech, actions, ambitions, time, talents, job, finances, and relationships will all be shaped by Jesus. Mature men allow God to grow them in all aspects.

Mature men not only walk with God in all aspects of their life, but they also stand for the things God stands for. In Ephesians 5:11-14, Paul is calling the Ephesian church to take a stand. There is nothing the enemy wants more than to push the church back into the shadows and to keep God's people silent. The church has been given three primary ways to impact the world for the glory of God: sanctification, service, and speech. Sanctification is the process of becoming more like Jesus. To grow in all aspects means that you have entered into the sanctification process. The world cannot ignore the transformation that God does in his people. The world can try to explain it away, but the world cannot ignore it.

The gift of service confuses our world that is steeped in selfishness. Christian service is rooted in love and sacrifice. When Christians serve others sacrificially, the world doesn't know how to deal with the selfless love and acts of grace. The church loves this way because that's the way Jesus demonstrated his love toward us. He laid down his life for ours, he was gentle and patient, he stood on truth, and he loved us unconditionally. Mature men must strive to serve the world like Jesus.

The world usually has no problem with these first two gifts that the church pours into the culture. It is the gift of speech that the world can't tolerate. It is the gift of speech that the church struggles with as well. Christians are called to take a stand and speak for what is true. To take a stand for what is true, we must know the truth. The truth isn't hidden from us; it is in plain sight. The Word of God is the book of truth, and Jesus Christ is the man of truth.

Mature men are trained in the Word of God so that they will be able to discern the truth from the lies. In Ephesians 4:14, Paul tells the church that they are no longer children carried about by every wind of doctrine. As we grow into mature Christian men, we need to have a firm foundation of doctrinal truth so that we won't be shaken by the wind of false doctrine, the trickery of men, or the crafty schemes of the devil.

Ephesians 5:11 calls Christians to expose the unfruitful deeds of darkness. Maturing Christians understand the importance of shining a light into the shadows of life so that all things are visible. The world will be resistant to this light; therefore, the world will be resistant to you. Jesus told his disciples that they would face trouble in this world because he faced trouble. Many people overlooked how Jesus' ministry of teaching, preaching, and miracles transformed lives. There were many people who disagreed with his message about repentance and belief. They constantly tried to quiet him, and eventually, they crucified Him.

Jesus' early disciples faced a similar scenario. In Acts 4, Peter and John heal a man, and they begin preaching about Jesus. Some people were greatly disturbed, so they had Peter and John arrested. Consider what happens next.

Acts 4:16-17:

"What shall we do with these men? For the fact that a noteworthy miracle has taken place through them is apparent to all who live in Jerusalem, and we cannot deny it. But so that it will not spread any further among the people, let us warn them to speak no longer to any man in this name."

Don't forget that Peter and John were fishermen by trade. Now, they are servants of Christ taking a bold stand to proclaim the gospel at all costs! Notice that the council says, "We cannot deny that a noteworthy miracle has taken place but let us warn them not to speak in the name of Jesus anymore." We should expect resistance, and we need to expect people to be disturbed by the message of the gospel. If we are not facing any resistance, we may not be speaking the truth like Jesus.

Mature men will not be silent about proclaiming Jesus' crucifixion and resurrection from the dead. Do not be so consumed with the trials of sharing your faith that you miss out on the joy of sharing your faith. Consider what took place before Peter and John were arrested. Acts 4:4

says, "But many of those who had heard the message believed; and the number of the men came to be about five thousand." When Peter and John were released from prison, do you think they were silent? Absolutely not! Why would you and I forfeit in freedom what these men would not abandon in prison? Mature men are sanctified servants who will not stand by silently holding on to the message of light in a dark and dying world.

How can we measure our Christian maturity? Many people believe that maturity comes through years of experience, but that's not necessarily the case. People often reference Christian maturity as wisdom. Wisdom is also usually measured by years of experience. Paul calls the church in Ephesus to walk as wise men. How do we gain wisdom? How do we become spiritually mature men? After all, isn't that what the wise king Solomon told us to do? In Proverbs 4:5:

"Acquire wisdom! Acquire understanding!
Do not forget nor turn away from the words of my mouth. "Do not forsake her, and she will

guard you; Love her, and she will watch over you.

"The beginning of wisdom is: Acquire wisdom;

And with all your acquiring, get understanding.

"Prize her, and she will exalt you."

We get the idea that we are to acquire wisdom. Just when we think we are going to get some instruction about how to gain wisdom, he says the beginning of wisdom is to acquire wisdom. Isn't that frustrating! That is how a lot of men feel when they hear things like, "Mature in your faith, acquire wisdom, and be the spiritual leader of your home." These statements are very vague. We need more specific instruction; we need to be able to identify what success looks like. How do we know if we are maturing? How do we know if we are gaining wisdom? How do we know we are leading well? I encourage you to begin measuring maturity, wisdom, and leadership by how obedient you are to the commands of God. The first part of Proverbs 4 tells us that the father wants to pass down his wisdom, but he knows that wisdom is only gained through obeying instruction.

The book of Proverbs and the book of

Deuteronomy gives us great insight on gaining wisdom and growing in maturity.

Proverbs 4:1-4:

> "Hear, O sons, the instruction of a father,
> And give attention that you may gain
> understanding, For I give you sound teaching;
> Do not abandon my instruction. When I was a son
> to my father, tender and the only son in the sight
> of my mother, then he taught me and said to me,
> "Let your heart hold fast my words;
> Keep my commandments and live."

Deuteronomy 4:5-6:

> "See, I have taught you statutes and judgments
> just as the LORD my God commanded me, that
> you should do this in the land where you are
> entering to possess it. "So keep and do them, for
> that is your wisdom and your understanding in
> the sight of the peoples who will hear all these
> statutes and say, 'Surely this great nation is a wise
> and understanding people."

Maturing as a Christian man means that you simply take the next right step of obedience in your walk of faith. To know the instruction and commands of the Father, to keep them, and do them— that is your wisdom.

Paul highlights the role of the family in Ephesians 5:22. He talks about the role and the responsibility of the Christ-centered man in the home. Paul understood that if the church was going to be healthy, it would start with the home being healthy. If the homes were going to be healthy, then the men would need to have a clear understanding of their role as husbands and fathers. Men are to be the leaders in the home. Men have a position of authority that should be evident in their service and sacrifice. In other words, if God has given you a wife, he has given you the privilege of serving and nourishing her. If he has given you children, he expects you to lead them well and train them in the Word of God.

Paul described marriage by placing it side by side with the ministry of Jesus and his relationship with the church. Paul understood that marriage was given by God so that the world would always have a physical representation of the spiritual reality of God's desired relationship with humanity. In Ephesians 5:21-33, Paul goes back and forth, talking about the role of the husband and wife.

The husband is to be like Christ:

- Christ is the head of the church
- Christ loves the church
- Christ sanctifies the church
- Christ sacrifices for the church
- Christ nourishes and cherishes the church
- Christ is one with the church

The wife is to be as the church:

- The church surrenders to Christ
- The church adores Christ
- The church is holy and blameless through Christ
- The church respects Christ
- The church is one with Christ

If we go through these truths and replace the word Christ with husband and church with wife, we will see what Paul is trying to tell us in Ephesians 5. Then, and only then, we will begin to have a better understanding of marriage and its mission. What Paul describes in Ephesians 5 is God's outline for marriage.

Have you ever considered what is the purpose of your marriage? If you men are anything like me, you work with more diligence if you fully understand the purpose for which you are working. I don't mind building things, but I like to have a picture or a blueprint for what I am doing instead of aimlessly nailing boards together and hoping that it becomes something useful. I don't think God intends for us to live aimlessly in our marriage. I believe that God not only wants to reveal himself in our marriages, but he also wants to use our marriages to make a kingdom impact in the world.

Paul was concerned about people's understanding of marriage in the community of Ephesus and within the church. I am also worried about people's views of marriage in my community and my church. We live in a world where marriage has been under attack, and worldly perspectives and ungodly examples are undercutting the very foundation of a Biblical marriage. It's time for Christian men and women to be clear not just on the meaning of marriage but also on the purpose of marriage. If God compares marriage to Christ and his love for the church, it would be wise for us to consider the church's goal and purpose in the world.

The church is defined as the body of Christ. The body of Christ is to be God's representative in the world: a beacon of truth and holiness that points others to Christ by fulfilling the great commission. In Matthew 28:18-20, the church is called to, "Go and make disciples of all nations baptizing them in the name of the Father, Son and Holy Spirit, teaching them all that I commanded you." If this is the mission of the church, then it is also the mission of your marriage. Not many husbands are talking with their wives about what it means for them to be a witness for Christ. Marriages are suffering because people don't understand the purpose of marriage. You and your wife need to be on mission together. When you take your vows before God and before his church, you are vowing to live under his leadership. His leadership always leads to his mission and his glory. Who are you and your spouse praying for, how are you serving, and to whom are you teaching the gospel? You see, if we lack this mindset within marriage, we will lose our children to the world instead of them growing up seeing what a godly marriage does for the kingdom and what it means to be a family on mission for Christ. I encourage you to engage your family in the church and be on mission. Mature men and their wives will train their children in the Word of God by living it out and teaching it to them. Men, be wise and mature in your faith by taking the next right step within your marriage and family.

SCRIPTURE READING – EPHESIANS 4:11-16

11   And He gave some as apostles, and some as prophets, and some as evangelists, and some as pastors and teachers,

12   for the equipping of the saints for the work of service, to the building up of the body of Christ;

13   until we all attain to the unity of the faith, and of the knowledge of the Son of God, to a mature man, to the measure of the stature which belongs to the fullness of Christ.

14   As a result, we are no longer to be children, tossed here and there by waves and carried about by every wind of doctrine, by the trickery of men, by craftiness in deceitful scheming;

15   but speaking the truth in love, we are to grow up in all aspects into Him who is the head, even Christ,

16   from whom the whole body, being fitted and held together by what every joint supplies, according to the proper working of each individual part, causes the growth of the body for the building up of itself in love.

DISCUSSION QUESTIONS

What are some key elements of spiritual growth we see in these verses?

Have you ever thought that you needed the body of Christ to help you grow in maturity?

Have you considered that the body of Christ needs you to reach maturity in faith?

What are some other aspects of growing in maturity in Christ?

What is the impact of Christian maturity on your marriage and family?

ADDITIONAL RESOURCES

10

PREPARED MEN

FOR BODILY DISCIPLINE IS ONLY OF LITTLE PROFIT,
BUT GODLINESS IS PROFITABLE FOR ALL THINGS,
SINCE IT HOLDS PROMISE FOR THE PRESENT LIFE AND
ALSO FOR THE LIFE TO COME.

1 TIMOTHY 4:8

Are you ready for what lies ahead? It is good to
have a heart that is ready, but it is better to have a ready
heart that is prepared. In the 1993 film *Rudy*, the world was
introduced to Daniel Rudy Ruettiger, who stood five feet,
seven inches tall and weighed 165 pounds. Rudy had a
dream of playing football at Notre Dame. No one had more
heart than Rudy, but he was discouraged because of his
size and his learning disability. After high school, Rudy went
to work at a factory, where he met a friend who believed in
him. There is one scene in which Rudy is having dinner with
his friend, and Rudy is wearing a Notre Dame letterman

jacket. Rudy asked, "How does it look?" His friend said, "You were born to wear that jacket." What inspiring words!

Sadly, his friend was later killed in a tragic accident. Rudy recounted those days in an interview, and he said, "His death gave me a reason – a reason to live again and a reason to chase my dreams." Rudy quit work to pursue his dream. After being denied entrance to the school several times, he was finally accepted into Notre Dame. That was only part of his dream. He walked onto the practice football team, where he played his heart out on defense for two seasons. The last game was approaching, and Rudy was losing hope that he would actually get to play for the Notre Dame team. His hope was restored when two players entered the coach's office, and they asked if they could exchange places with Rudy for this one last game. The coach gave in to their request, and Rudy dressed out for his first and only game as a football player for Notre Dame. The story didn't end there. At the end of the game, Notre Dame was winning, and word got out that Rudy, who had been a faithful practice team player, had dressed out.

As the crowd chanted his name, Rudy goes in on defense to play the last twenty-seven seconds of the game. He makes a phenomenal tackle to end his football career. The movie wasn't about winning a football game; it was about winning at life. For believers in Christ, we also have one whose death should motivate us to live and fulfill the calling that God has on our lives. We, too, have one who became our substitute so that we could have a place on the team. His name is Jesus.

It's going to take more than just desire and heart to live up to what God has for us. In one interview, Rudy said, "I wouldn't have ever made that tackle if I had not spent time preparing... I was ready for that moment. I didn't know I was going to get it, but you have got to be ready for it." Don't overlook Rudy's two years of faithful practice where he was preparing for *the hour* or *those twenty-seven seconds*. There wasn't anyone on the field more prepared to make the tackle than Rudy Ruettiger. He was ready, and he was prepared. When readiness is paired with preparedness, I believe we start to see the evidence of

God's greatness in and through our lives. In Ephesians 6:10-19, Paul uses the picture of a man putting on armor to prepare for battle. This is what we must do every day to be prepared for the task that God has for us.

Ready men have desire and motivation; ready men have heart. However, there have been a lot of ready men who haven't been prepared. Prepared men are ready in season and out of season, every minute, and every moment. They have put in the work and have been trained. They continue to train for whatever lies ahead. They know their strengths and weaknesses; they are laser-focused, prepared as a soldier ready for battle. They know their equipment, their skills, and they are ready for whatever challenge they may face. They are strengthened and protected by the full armor of God. Men, you were born to wear this armor. Prepared men stand firm against the schemes of the evil one. They are gentle, patient, and tolerant with people in this world because they know they are fighting against the spiritual forces of wickedness in the heavenly places.

Prepared men are protected from head to toe because their identity is hidden in Christ. Their shield of faith not only protects their areas of weakness, but it also protects their brothers next to them from every flaming arrow of the enemy. Prepared men do not wait for the battle to come to them. They wage war against the enemy of lies with the sword of truth. You see, prepared men are counted on. They are not easily swayed by resistance or disturbances. They can quickly identify the enemy. They have unveiled and exposed his tactics. God is interested in preparing men for every battle that is to come. Are we prepared for the battle? Are we preparing the next generation?

While Paul was traveling on his missionary journeys, he was led to a young man named Timothy. Timothy became a young disciple of Christ and Paul's right-hand man in ministry. He was there during the training sessions in Ephesus before Paul sent him away to minister in Macedonia. Paul sent him to many other churches to train him and equip him for the work of ministry. Notice what Paul told Timothy in his last letter to him.

2 Timothy 2:1-4:

> "You, therefore, my son, be strong in the grace that is in Christ Jesus. The things which you have heard from me in the presence of many witnesses, entrust these to faithful men who will be able to teach others also. Suffer hardship with me, as a good soldier of Christ Jesus. No soldier in active service entangles himself in the affairs of everyday life, so that he may please the one who enlisted him as a soldier."

Paul understood being on mission for God as a soldier fulfilling his duty in active service. A soldier in those days didn't have a civilian life and military life. Paul told Timothy not to entangle himself in the everyday affairs of life. You and I must also have this same mindset. Prepared men know they belong to Christ first and foremost. They have matured by growing up in all aspects into Christ, and they have put off the old ways of the world. Their lives are led by a new commander, the Holy Spirit, who dwells within. They know who has called them and to what they have been called. They have been trained and tested. They have proven to be men of wisdom and have been found ready to wage war. They know the family is under attack, so they fight for their wives, their children, their children's children, and their brothers and sisters and their children. Prepared men fight for the sake of all humanity so that those who are dead in their trespasses and sins may become alive in Christ through his mercy and grace. They fight to save the very ones who come against them. Why would they do that? They fight because Christ fought for them and won the victory for them while they were hostile toward God.

Notice what else Paul told Timothy in 2 Timothy 2:1-2. "The things which you have heard from me in the presence of many witnesses, entrust these to faithful men, who will be able to teach others also." There are four generations of faithful men represented in that one sentence: Paul teaching Timothy, Timothy teaching faithful men, and faithful men teaching the future generation.

Prepared men are ready to train the next generation of warriors for the kingdom. Prepared men prepare others.

A friend of mine was working caring for a patient, and she posted this on her social media page:

> "Yesterday, after a patient made a comment, 'I'm thankful I'm not raising young children today,' I hung my head and gave the response of 'yeah, I know what you mean.' I got to my car and was immediately convicted- like the Lord was asking me 'Girl, why are you not standing firm in My victory?! I've already overcome the world! The joy of the Lord is your strength!' In a chaotic world, we can stand firm with confidence in a God who is sovereign over all time and all things!"

I love that God convicted her of having a defeated mindset. The reality is, we are training warriors for the kingdom. The enemy tries to rule over us with discouragement, but we are no longer under his command. Prepared parents prepare their children to live a victorious life in a world full of discouragement.

As men, we are called to train other men. This will take time, and it will take intentionality, but it will be worth it. It's not enough to just have a ready heart; we must be trained and prepared to face the war at hand. There are a lot of *ready* men, and when we start *preparing* ready men, we will see God's kingdom reign on earth as it is in heaven.

By the way, Scripture tells us that Timothy became the overseer for many of the churches that Paul helped establish. Historical tradition tells us that Timothy was likely the overseer of the churches in Ephesus as well. Only eternity will tell of the impact that our intentional training of others will have over the course of time. Part of being a disciple of Jesus is discipling others in the faith.

STUDY SESSION 10 – PREPARED MEN

SCRIPTURE READING – EPHESIANS 6:10-17

10   Finally, be strong in the Lord and in the strength of His might.

11   Put on the full armor of God, so that you will be able to stand firm against the schemes of the devil.

12   For our struggle is not against flesh and blood, but against the rulers, against the powers, against the world forces of this darkness, against the spiritual forces of wickedness in the heavenly places.

13   Therefore, take up the full armor of God, so that you will be able to resist in the evil day, and having done everything, to stand firm.

14   Stand firm therefore, HAVING GIRDED YOUR LOINS WITH TRUTH, and HAVING PUT ON THE BREASTPLATE OF RIGHTEOUSNESS,

15   and having shod YOUR FEET WITH THE PREPARATION OF THE GOSPEL OF PEACE;

16   in addition to all, taking up the shield of faith with which you will be able to extinguish all the flaming arrows of the evil one.

17   And take THE HELMET OF SALVATION, and the sword of the Spirit, which is the word of God.

DISCUSSION QUESTIONS

Why do you think Paul closes his letter to the Ephesians talking about the armor of God?

What is the difference in being ready and being prepared?

Have you ever been involved in a discipleship training process that made a significant difference? What did it consist of?

What is the difference in fighting with the strength of His might versus your own?

ADDITIONAL RESOURCES

11

PRAYING MEN

THE EFFECTIVE PRAYER OF A RIGHTEOUS MAN
CAN ACCOMPLISH MUCH.
JAMES 5:16b

We spend most of our days talking to ourselves. From the moment we wake up until the moment we lie down, we are usually talking to ourselves about work, thinking through a problem, figuring out what we are going to eat, or planning our next day off. If we can implement one small shift into our daily conversation, it can have a huge impact on our lives. You see, the enemy works in our minds because that is the secret place. He wants to consume our minds with obligations, selfish ambitions, and negative thoughts that will lead to frustration and discouragement. Without even realizing it throughout the day, the enemy has jumped into the conversation that you have been having with yourself. This seems to be the case in Genesis 3 when Adam and Eve were enjoying their day in the garden. The enemy came and began to negotiate with them and tempt them. It was subtle but effective. We must learn to identify the conversation of the enemy, and the best way to shut down the enemy's conversation is to start a conversation with God.

When we learn to include God in our daily conversation with ourselves, we will learn to walk with God and listen to his voice. Seek God's opinion, ask God for clarity, and plead for God's help. Seeking God continually in prayer is vital for maturing in our faith and being prepared for whatever lies ahead. Paul says it well in 1 Thessalonians 5:17, "Pray without ceasing." It is not a coincidence that he talks about prayer as one of the offensive weapons that we are to use as we go to battle in this life. "With all prayer and petition pray at all times in the Spirit" (Eph 6:18). Prayer not only gets us through the battles of every day; prayer is how we battle for our brothers and sisters and those who are lost!

When I was just starting to follow Jesus, my youth pastor would take us to a campground for a winter retreat.

Every year, we would have this time when he would teach us to pray for other people. He had us write our prayer request on a piece of paper, place the papers in the bonfire, and ask God to take over and take control of our prayer request. I didn't think much about it at the time. I knew I wanted my brothers to know Jesus, so I just wrote their names on the paper. The next year rolled around, and I wrote my brothers' names down again. This time, it was different. My heart was truly burdened for them, and I remember sharing with others that I was concerned about their salvation. I desperately wanted God to step into their lives.

Several years later, my middle brother gave me a groomsmen's gift for being in his wedding. It was one of the greatest gifts I have ever received. It was a Bass Pro Shop gift card! I know what you are thinking... a Bass Pro gift card is one of the greatest gifts you have ever received? It was the note that was stuck to the back of the gift card that struck my spirit. The note read, "Because you prayed for me when I was lost, I love you." These simple words changed me forever. It was in that moment that the memories of those nights around the bonfire at winter retreat came flooding back into my mind. Prayer is how we fight our battles, and prayer is how we fight for others as well. My brother knew I had prayed for him; but more importantly, God knew I prayed for him. God was gracious in allowing me to see the answer to my prayers.

If you have been praying for something for years, remain steadfast in prayer and never give up. Know that your prayers are accomplishing much even when you haven't received an answer. Prayer builds our faith and our trust in God. Prayer tells God that we rely on him. Through prayer and the periods of time when we are waiting for answers, God is transforming us. If you spend all of your days talking to yourself, let me warn you; the enemy is making his way into that conversation. I encourage you to talk to the Father. James 4:7 tells us, "Submit therefore to God. Resist the devil, and he will flee from you." Pray for yourself, pray for others, and make sure you have some prayer warriors praying for you.

Throughout my life, I have had several prayer warriors: people who prayed for my salvation, people who pray over the ministries where I am serving, and people who pray over my marriage and my family. I am often reminded about their prayers in times of weakness and temptation. Recently, I went through a difficult time. In that season, I had numerous friends reach out to encourage me and say that they were praying for me. The remarkable thing about this was that these friends did not even know that I was going through a difficult season. God sure uses the prayers of his people to shape us into who he wants us to be. Never underestimate the power of your prayers as you lift them up to the all-powerful God who hears. Prepared men know how to battle in prayer.

STUDY SESSION 11 – PRAYING MEN

SCRIPTURE READING – EPHESIANS 6:18-20

18   With all prayer and petition pray at all times in the Spirit, and with this in view, be on the alert with all perseverance and petition for all the saints,

19   and pray on my behalf, that utterance may be given to me in the opening of my mouth, to make known with boldness the mystery of the gospel,

20   for which I am an ambassador in chains; that in proclaiming it I may speak boldly, as I ought to speak.

DISCUSSION QUESTIONS

Paul lists prayer as one of the offensive weapons of the armor of God. Have you ever considered prayer as a weapon?

Do you have a set aside time to pray each day?

Do you find yourself talking to God throughout the day?

What does Paul mean when he says, pray with all prayer and petition?

What is the most obvious way that you have seen God answer prayer in your life?

What is one prayer that you want God to answer?

ADDITIONAL RESOURCES

READY OR NOT

THEREFORE, PREPARE YOUR MINDS FOR ACTION,
KEEP SOBER IN SPIRIT, FIX YOUR HOPE COMPLETELY
ON THE GRACE TO BE BROUGHT TO YOU AT THE
REVELATION OF JESUS CHRIST.

1 PETER 1:13

I'd like for us to turn our attention to Paul's
farewell to the church in Ephesus. Be mindful that these
events take place before Paul wrote his letter to the church
in Ephesus. Paul had left Ephesus, but he sent for the
church leaders to meet him for some last remarks and
encouragement.

Last remarks should be highly valued, because
they are likely well thought through and come directly from
the heart. Paul knew that he probably would not see these
believers again, so his last words were strong with passion
and emotion. Paul trusted that God was going to finish the
work that he had started, even if Paul wasn't going to see

the fruit in his lifetime. Paul began his closing remarks by sharing his commitment and calling to humbly preach the gospel with boldness, not shrinking back in the face of adversity. He says in Acts 20:27, "For I did not shrink back from declaring to you the whole purpose of God." This was meant to embolden the believers in Ephesus so that they would continue the work no matter what. Paul then moves to a word of warning, and it's a warning we must consider as well.

When you get to know people and become familiar with the culture they are entrenched in, you can see the potential struggles they might face in following Jesus. Notice what Paul goes on to say in Acts 20:28. "Be on guard for yourselves and for all the flock." He was telling the church leaders to remember that they were overseers of the church, which Christ purchased with his own blood. Paul was fearful that troubles would arise within the leadership of the church. He said that he knew that savage wolves would arise from within, and the flock would suffer. Pastors and church leaders should heed these words of warning. Church members should heed this warning as well. Paul then writes, "I commend you to God, and to the word of His grace, which is able to build you up and to give you the inheritance among all those who are sanctified" (Acts 20:32). In other words, Paul said, I have done what God has called me to do here; now, may God continue the work that he began.

After almost ten years of ministry serving at New Zion Baptist Church, God called me to another place of ministry. We had built our lives with those friends, and we strived to carry God's Word into that community. The people that poured into us and cared for our family were in that church. Leaving that community was hard for our family. After a couple of years of being away, my wife and I were invited back to preach and lead worship at the homecoming celebration. I don't think I was fully prepared for what God was going to do in my heart that day. It was so good to see all the families and students that we had shared life with for those nine-plus years. B.J., one of the young men that I had invested in, was helping lead worship that day. B.J. strummed the guitar and began to sing the words, "God is able. He will never fail. He is Almighty God." I began to weep with tears of joy and glory for what God had done, was doing, and was going to do in that faith family. God reminded me that it is a privilege and honor to serve his kingdom and his people. May we never forget that.

Paul was dedicated to the church that God called him to serve. Paul was willing to give his life for the church that Christ purchased with his blood. You see, prepared men live for the things Christ died for. They are ready and prepared, because they know that time is fleeting. As the church leaders in Ephesus led Paul to the ship to set sail for what Paul knew would be a difficult season of ministry, they wept and prayed and embraced one another. Paul viewed the churches that he served as his joy and his crown (Philippians 4:1). He wanted there to be evidence of his faithfulness to God through the influence of his ministry.

What will be the evidence of our faithfulness? Better yet, *who* will be the evidence of our faithfulness? There is no greater joy in life than to serve his kingdom by preparing others to live faithfully for Jesus. You see, the church belongs to Jesus, and if Jesus is the leader of the local church, we ought to joyfully serve in the local church. Don't live your life without experiencing this joy-filled service.

There is one last warning to the church in Ephesus, and it will be our final warning. Jesus writes personal letters to churches in Revelation 2 and 3. We should carefully read those letters and apply all those truths to our churches. What did he say specifically to the church in Ephesus? After giving the church praise because of their faithfulness to the truth, Revelation 2:4 says, "But I have this against you, that you have left your first love. Therefore, remember where you have fallen, and repent and do the deeds you did at first." The warning is not to forget and to always remember. Men fall and churches lose their influence because they fail to remember. Never forget

123

your first love, the one who loved you and gave himself up for you. When God created man, he created him with the name "male", which in Hebrew means "remembering one." May we never forget our first love, and may we live for Jesus in every moment of every hour knowing that *the hour* may come at any given moment. Are you ready or not? May we be found ready and prepared for all that God has in store.

STUDY SESSION 12 – READY OR NOT

SCRIPTURE READING – ACTS 20:17-21

17   From Miletus he sent to Ephesus and called to him
      the elders of the church.

18   And when they had come to him, he said to them,
      "You yourselves know, from the first day that I set
      foot in Asia, how I was with you the whole time,

19   serving the Lord with all humility and with tears
      and with trials which came upon me through the
      plots of the Jews;

20   how I did not shrink from declaring to you
      anything that was profitable, and teaching you
      publicly and from house to house,

21   solemnly testifying to both Jews and Greeks of
      repentance toward God and faith in our Lord Jesus
      Christ.

DISCUSSION QUESTIONS

Paul's last words to the elders in the church of Ephesus serve as his legacy. What would be your last words to your church?

What will be the evidence of your faithfulness? Better yet, *who* will be the evidence of your faithfulness?

What are some practical things you can do to continue to invest the gospel in others?

As men of faith, will you commit to consistently testifying of repentance toward God and faith in our Lord Jesus Christ?

ADDITIONAL RESOURCES

For additional sermons and Bible study resources,

scan the QR code.

ACKNOWLEDGEMENTS

I want to thank my friends and family who read through this work and encouraged me to see it through to completion. A special thanks to Linda Pierce, Jeremy Gibbs, and Ryan Reeves who proofed and offered suggestions. To my First Baptist Church Lake family, I am grateful for the way you cover me in prayer and encourage me to continue to seek Jesus. Thanks to the men who have encouraged and trained me to be a disciple of Jesus. To my wife Dru, thank you for your love and support. Your pursuit of Jesus motivates and encourages me to honor Jesus every moment of every hour.

Made in the USA
Columbia, SC
28 February 2025

54544358R00074